T0113667

God,
My Strength

Elisa Tiffany Maxine Rahming

WESTBOW
PRESS®
A DIVISION OF THOMAS NELSON
& ZONDERVAN

WestBow Press books may be ordered through
booksellers or by contacting:

WestBow Press
A Division of Thomas Nelson & Zondervan
1663 Liberty Drive
Bloomington, IN 47403
www.westbowpress.com
1 (866) 928-1240

Scripture taken from the New King James Version®. Copyright ©
1982 by Thomas Nelson. Used by permission. All rights reserved.

ISBN: 978-1-9736-9717-6 (sc)
ISBN: 978-1-9736-9718-3 (e)

Print information available on the last page.

WestBow Press rev. date: 8/27/2020

To *you,* each person who reads this book, so that you will find God's strength for each new day and for the journey ahead.

CONTENTS

PREFACE

God, My Strength was birthed by my desire to share encouraging and inspirational scripture verses and commentary with family and friends. During my morning devotional time, I would read God's Word and write what He impressed upon me from the scripture. I would then share it via text messaging and social media. Sharing God's inspiration gave me further inspiration and encouragement. It is true that as we refresh others, according to Proverbs 11:25, we ourselves are refreshed.

I also shared with others to help them on their Christian journey, to strengthen their relationships with God. My personal mission statement is "sharing insights, principles, and truths to encourage dreams and closer relationships with God and others." And as I shared with others and lived out my purpose, I sensed God's pleasure and felt fulfilled.

A friend once asked me if I was saving my messages for a book, and that planted a seed. Eventually, I compiled some of the messages that particularly focused on God's strength and that I had sent to family and friends, and I expanded those messages to become what you see here today.

It was a beautiful journey led by God, and every time I reread His Word and His inspiration given to me in this book, I am once again refreshed, encouraged, inspired, and strengthened. My prayer is that you too will be refreshed, encouraged, inspired, and strengthened upon reading and rereading this book. God is truly our strength.

INTRODUCTION

God is truly my strength, our strength, and this book reveals that in multiple ways. Scripture was selectively chosen by what encouraged and strengthened me as I enjoyed personal devotional time with God. And I hope and pray that as you delve into the pages, whether it is during your devotional time or otherwise, that you too will be encouraged and strengthened.

Over the years, I've come to understand and learn the importance of having personal devotional time with our Savior and Lord. He draws us to Himself every day and longs to spend quality time with us. He delights in us, and as we spend time with Him on a daily basis, we find ourselves delighting more and more in Him and in the time spent with Him. Without a daily relationship with Him, I am powerless. With a daily relationship with Him, I am empowered and strengthened by Him. Jesus says, "I am the vine, you are the branches. He who abides in Me, and I in him, bears much fruit; for without Me you can do nothing" (John 15:5). Abiding in Jesus, daily living in and connecting with Him, is of utmost importance to our Christian journey. I pray that today you will commit, or recommit, to spending daily devotional time with our Lord and King.

DAY 1

God's Strength in Our Weaknesses

And He said to me, My grace is sufficient for you,
for My strength is made perfect in weakness.
—2 Corinthians 12:9

How can we take hold of God's strength and have it manifested in our lives? Acknowledge our weaknesses. Acknowledge that we are nothing without Him. Acknowledge our need for Him. His strength is made perfect in our weaknesses.

When we acknowledge that we need Him over and above everything and everyone else, something inside us draws us closer to Him and His ability to strengthen us and empower us. When we acknowledge that we need Him even to breathe, we feel Him in every breath we take. We feel His strength, His power, and His love. He is strength, and we are weakness. And that's okay. Because when He abides in us, His strength becomes our strength, even in our weaknesses.

Prayer: Lord, may we acknowledge our need for You every day, may we acknowledge our weaknesses, and may we embrace Your strength. For in You and with You, we are made strong in our weaknesses.

DAY 2

Inner Strength

That He would grant you, according to the riches
of His glory, to be strengthened with might
through His Spirit in the inner man, that Christ
may dwell in your hearts through faith.
—Ephesians 3:16–17

Paul is praying for God's supernatural strength for the Christians in Ephesus. He is praying for power. We can also pray for this same strength for ourselves and for others. Strength that will not wane. Strength that buoys up our spirits. Strength that fills us and renews us. Strength that lasts forever. Supernatural strength through the Holy Spirit that takes us to the last mile.

God desires to give us strength and power on a daily basis—strength and power that will fill our hearts to live for Him.

Prayer: Lord, may we be daily filled with Your strength.

DAY 3

God's Amazing Presence

And there were also many other things that
Jesus did, which if they were written one by one,
I suppose that even the world itself could not
contain the books that would be written.
—John 21:25

Amazing. And I could just imagine a light, healing touch; an encouraging word spoken; a look of compassion. The small things happening over and over. And then the big things: healing, preaching, sharing, and long conversations about salvation and character. The list could go on and on. What an amazing man Jesus was. What an amazing God He is. He is our God. He is our Lord. And He is there for us. Always. Whenever we're lost, we can reach out to Him. Whenever we're sad, we can reach out to Him. Whenever we're confused, we can reach out to Him. Whenever we need Him, He is there. Is it any wonder that we truly can seek Him daily for strength?

Prayer: Lord, may we truly understand how amazing You are and how full of strength You are. May we embrace Your strength and reach out to You every day.

DAY 4

God Is with Us

But when the morning had come, Jesus stood on the
shore; yet the disciples did not know that it was Jesus.
—John 21:4

Again Jesus is appearing to them post-resurrection. He
doesn't want to leave them without sufficient encouragement
and strength to handle the tasks ahead of them. But initially,
they don't even know that it is Him. They are unaware of
His very near presence in their lives. So they struggle on
their own to make things happen—with no success. But
when Jesus gets involved, they have success and they become
aware of His presence.

Are we like that sometimes? Do we struggle on our
own to make things happen? Do we struggle in our own
weaknesses without being aware of His very near presence
in our lives? Jesus is always near, and with Him, there is help
and strength for each new day.

Prayer: Lord, may we always be aware of Your ever-present
help and strength for our lives today and every day.

DAY 5

God's Peace

Peace be unto you.
—John 20:26

This is the third time since His resurrection that He is pronouncing peace on His disciples. He knew they needed it. Not just quiet. But peace. His peace.

He knows we need it. He knows the chaos in our lives. He knows the ups and downs we go through. He knows everything. And so He said to me, "May My peace be in your life continually. May you daily seek after Me and receive My strength, My power, My love, My peace." We can rest assured that if we are willing, we will receive His peace and His strength.

Prayer: Lord, we pray for Your peace that surpasses all understanding. Please fill us afresh every day with Your supernatural peace.

DAY 6

Empowering Love

The Lord your God in your midst, the Mighty One, will
save; He will rejoice over you with gladness, He will quiet
you with His love, He will rejoice over you with singing.
—Zephaniah 3:17

God's love empowers us. God's love strengthens us. God's
love quiets the fear in our hearts. God's love rejuvenates us.
God's love never fails.

When we allow ourselves to bask in God's love, powerful
things can happen. When we base our identities on who He
is and who we are in Him, life has meaning and purpose.
When we love others as God loves us, we are empowered to
fulfill our callings. May we daily feel the strength that God's
love gives.

Prayer: Lord, we long to bask in Your love today and every
day. Fill us with Your love, fill us with Your strength, and
may we love others as You do.

DAY 7

God's Love

For the Father Himself loves you, because you have loved
Me, and have believed that I came forth from God.
—John 16:27

The Father Himself says He loves us. He wants a relationship
with us. He wants to spend time with us. He wants to
strengthen us. He wants to be there for us. He wants us. But
He will not force us. He has given us the freedom to choose,
and He will continue to allow us this liberty. And at the same
time, He will continue to draw us to Himself with hopes that
we will choose Him.

He loves us more than we can ever imagine. And His
love is there to strengthen us. But we have to receive His love;
we have to accept His love; we have to embrace His love so
that it can have its fullest impact in our lives. His love can
strengthen us if we allow Him.

Prayer: Lord, may we daily receive Your love and shower
Your love on others. May we be daily strengthened with
Your love.

DAY 8

Lingering with God

But Mary stood outside by the tomb weeping, and
as she wept she stooped down and looked into the
tomb... She turned around and saw Jesus standing
there, and did not know that it was Jesus.
—John 20:11, 14

Mary lingered a little longer than Peter and John did at the
tomb. She spent just a bit more time seeking God. And she
was rewarded. She saw Jesus. And His presence strengthened
her and encouraged her to share the good news to the others.
He is alive! And because she lingered awhile in His presence,
she was strengthened.

When we linger awhile in His presence, we are rewarded.
We are strengthened and encouraged to continue on.

Prayer: Lord, thank You for Your presence. Thank You for
Your strength. May we daily linger awhile in Your presence
and receive Your strength.

DAY 9

Courage

Have I not commanded you? Be strong and of good
courage; do not be afraid, nor be dismayed, for the
Lord your God is with you wherever you go.
—Joshua 1:9

We can be strong only through the strength of Jesus. He can
fill us with His strength and encouragement so that we can
be courageous. By ourselves, we are weak. Even when we feel
strong, we are weak. But in Him and through His strength,
we can be truly strong, physically, mentally, and emotionally.

We can be of good courage because He has conquered
the world. We can be of good cheer because He is with us
wherever we go. We can release our fears to Him because
He is trustworthy. He is the Lord our God who is with us
wherever we go.

Prayer: Lord, may we reach out to You for Your strength,
today and every day, for Your courage. Through You, we are
truly more than conquerors.

DAY 10

God Is Our Refuge in Chaos

God is our refuge and strength, a very present help in
trouble. Therefore we will not fear, even though the
earth be removed, and though the mountains be carried
into the midst of the sea; though its waters roar and be
troubled, though the mountains shake with its swelling.
—Psalm 46:1–3

There may be total chaos within ourselves and in our lives,
but we still don't need to fear. God reminds us that even
within chaos, He is present. Waters roaring and mountains
shaking—chaos! Whether real or imagined. And in the
midst of chaos, He is there.

But is He really? What about God being a God of order
and not confusion? This is true. He delights in order and
perfection. But He is always with us, even in our disordered
and imperfect lives. He has promised that He will never leave
us nor forsake us. And we can rely on Him and His Word.
He will strengthen us daily. He will replace our fear with
courage, boldness, and a renewed trust in Him if we allow
Him. He will be our strength. He will be our help.

Prayer: Lord, thank You for always being with us even in the
midst of chaos. Thank You for Your strength and defense.
Thank You.

DAY 11

God Always Hears Us

Out of the depths I have cried to You, O
Lord; Lord, hear my voice! Let Your ears be
attentive to the voice of my supplication.
—Psalm 130:1–2

Being heard, listened to, by family and friends encourages us to keep on going. Being heard, listened to, by our heavenly Father gives us supernatural courage and strength for our journeys ahead. We can breathe a sigh of relief and release when we cry out to God. And we can know that when we cry out to Him, He hears us. He has promised that He will be attentive to our cries.

What a mighty God we serve. He loves us, He cares for us, He helps us, and He listens to us. He is there for us all the time, giving us strength, giving us love, and giving us everything we need.

Prayer: Lord, thank You for hearing our cries. May we never stop crying out to You; may we always reach out to You every day in every way.

DAY 12

Trusting God

Blessed is the man who trusts in the Lord, and whose
hope is the Lord. For he shall be like a tree planted
by the waters, which spreads out its roots by the
river, and will not fear when heat comes; but its leaf
will be green, and will not be anxious in the year
of drought, nor will cease from yielding fruit.
—Jeremiah 17:7–8

Love and trust are the opposite of fear and anxiety. When
we love as our Lord loves and totally trust Him, fear has no
place to exist and grow. Trusting Him is the key. Believing
Him is important. Hoping in Him and for Him is essential.
When we trust Him, we will be strengthened. We will also
be strengthened by God's love for us.

Through God's love, through trusting in Him, we can
be as strong as a tree that digs in its roots even further as
the storms come, the rains, the wind, the heat, the drought,
anything, but still it stands. We can stand strong in the
strength of our Lord.

Prayer: Lord, may we daily learn to trust You and expand
our "trust muscles" in the little things and in the big things.

DAY 13

God's Help

Fear not, for I am with you; be not dismayed, for I am
your God. I will strengthen you, yes, I will help you,
I will uphold you with My righteous right hand.
—Isaiah 41:10

He is our God. And we are His children. He will give us
strength for the journey ahead. He will help us. He will lift
us up and carry us when needed. He will always be there
for us. He has promised. So we don't have to fear. We don't
have to wonder whether He'll be there handling things on
our behalf. We don't have to be concerned that He's not big
enough or strong enough or smart enough. He is everything
we need Him to be and more. And He's got everything under
control.

If we just trust Him, if we just open our hearts to Him,
let Him in, and let Him take control, He will. And He will
do for us more than we could ever have imagined. He is
with us. And He will give us His strength. Strength that we
can rely on, strength that we can count on, and strength for
each day ahead.

Prayer: Lord, may we look to You for strength—strength
in the good times and strength in the bad times. Your
supernatural strength.

DAY 14

God Is Our Hope

For I know the thoughts that I think toward
you, says the Lord, thoughts of peace and not
of evil, to give you a future and a hope.
—Jeremiah 29:11

Do we really know God? Do we really understand how much He loves us and how much He wants good things for us? I would suggest that sometimes we don't. Sometimes we allow the enemy's lies about our loving Lord to influence us into thinking that He doesn't care, that we're on our own, that we have to figure things out by ourselves, and that life is hopeless. But we can throw the enemy's lies back into his face. God does love and care for us. We are not on our own. We don't have to figure things out by ourselves. He has promised to lead and guide us.

We have hope! He is our hope and can fill our lives with hope. He is there for us, each and every day, to strengthen us along the way. We are not on our own. We are loved.

Prayer: Lord, please daily remind us of Your love and care. May we be filled with a hope in You that is so great that it overflows our days. Thank You for Your love.

DAY 15

Our Compassionate Father

Through the Lord's mercies we are not consumed,
because His compassions fail not. They are new
every morning; great is Your faithfulness.
—Lamentations 3:22–23

God is great, and He is faithful. He loves us more than
we'll ever know or understand. He loves us deeply. We
are His children, and He is merciful to us every day. "Our
righteousness is as filthy rags" (Isaiah 64:6). But every day we
experience His compassion, His grace, and His forgiveness.
And every day we are to extend His compassion, grace,
and forgiveness to others. Our family, our loved ones, our
colleagues, and our friends all need it.

His love gives us strength to go on. His love is
empowering. His love is wonderful. God is faithful. God is
great. God is amazing.

Prayer: Lord, thank You for Your amazing love. Thank You
for Your faithfulness. May we always be reminded of Your
love and compassion to us, every day.

DAY 16

Help in Our Trials

Beloved, do not be surprised at the fiery ordeal
which comes upon you to prove you, as though
something strange were happening to you.
—1 Peter 4:12

Wow. Do not be surprised. It's coming. And over and over again. But we have a Savior who steps in the gap for us. Who feels our pain for us and with us. Who holds our hands through the trial, through the storm, and through the fiery ordeal. Who provides courage and strength so that we can overcome.

He tells us to "be of good cheer, for I have overcome the world" (John 16:33). So yes, we will have hard times, but we can lean into His strength every day to get us through those hard times. We can know that He will be there for us, that He is there for us. All we have to do is reach out to Him.

Prayer: Lord, may we tap into Your strength every day.

DAY 17

God Is Able

Our God whom we serve is able.
—Daniel 3:17

To me, that says it all, and it reminds me of the lyrics "He's able, He's able, I know He's able, I know my Lord is able to carry me through." But not forgetting the next verse, 18, even if He doesn't do exactly what we want, He is still able and we will serve only Him.

God is able. He is able to carry us through. He is able to give us His strength. He is able to provide for us. He is able to do all things. He is able.

As we go from day to day, may we always be reminded that God is truly able. He is all-powerful and all-knowing and desires everything that is for our good and His glory. May we daily experience His power and ability to move mountains as we seek Him and serve Him daily.

Prayer: Lord, You are able. Thank You for seeing us through and giving us Your strength to keep on going.

DAY 18

God Is Good

The Lord is good, a stronghold in the day of trouble;
And He knows those who trust in Him.
—Nahum 1:7

Indeed the Lord is good. He can be trusted. Surely "no good thing will He withhold from those who love Him" (Psalm 84:11). We can rely on Him as He is our help in the time of trouble. He knows us and He loves us. He knows His own. And He is good.

May we daily trust in Him for everything. May we daily trust in Him for strength. He is our strength. He is our fortress. He is our rock. When troubles come, we can run to Him. Always. He will be there. We can rest in Him.

Prayer: Lord, You are good, and Your mercies endure forever. Thank You for being our rock. Please sustain us.

DAY 19

No Need to Fear

The Lord is my light and my salvation;
whom shall I fear? The Lord is the strength
of my life; of whom shall I be afraid?
—Psalm 27:1

With God, we have nothing to fear. With God, we have nothing to dread. With God, we have light, salvation, and strength. With God, we have everything we need. God *is*.

Without God, there can be no true strength for life. But with God, we have all the strength we need. Day by day. May we daily tap into this strength to sustain us and keep us going through this journey of life with all its ups and downs and all-arounds.

Prayer: Father, thank You for living in me. Thank You for choosing me. Thank You for strengthening me.

DAY 20

Strength to Face Challenges

The Lord God is my strength. He makes me like a deer that does not stumble so I can walk on the steep mountains.
—Habakkuk 3:19 (NCV)

God is my strength. He is your strength. In everything He is our strength. Whatever your "steep mountains" are, God's strength is greater. Whenever you're having hard and trying times, God's strength can more than cover them. We can face tomorrow's challenges with boldness by His strength.

May we daily live in the awareness of God's strength in our lives. May we rest in the assurance that He's got enough strength for us for today and tomorrow. May we live and love and learn, every day.

Prayer: Lord, thank You for going ahead of us and showing us the way. Thank You for guiding us down the right path. Thank You for Your strength.

DAY 21

Reliance on God

Cursed is the man who trusts in man and
makes flesh his strength, whose heart departs
from the Lord... Blessed is the man who trusts
in the Lord, and whose hope is the Lord.
—Jeremiah 17:5, 7

Trust. What a distinction between being cursed and being blessed based on where and in whom we put our trust. Trusting God gives us strength. Trusting humankind does not. Will you trust Him today?

May we trust and hope in God, seeking Him first above all else, daily. May we rely on Him first even when the temptation comes to rely on others.

Prayer: Lord, You are my strength. You can be trusted. Help me to trust in You.

DAY 22

Daily Hope in God

And now, Lord, what do I wait for? My hope is in you.
—Psalm 39:7

This is a short yet powerful verse. God is my everything. My hope, my trust, and my confidence are in Him. I wait on Him to guide me day by day. I daily wait for His wisdom and strength. I daily wait for Him.

Every day, reach out to God for His strength, and He will come through. Every day, reach out to God for guidance through the decisions of life, and He will come through. Every day, reach out to God for hope, and He will instill hope in you. Every day, reach out to Him, and you will not be disappointed.

Prayer: Dear Lord, we reach out to You today and every day. We hope in You. Thank You for reaching back. Thank You for reaching for us even before we reach to You.

DAY 23

God Is Greater

Be of good courage, and let us be strong for our
people and for the cities of our God. And may
the Lord do what is good in His sight.
—1 Chronicles 19:13

Be of good courage, for God who is with us is greater than
the enemy who is against us. We can rely on Him to always
do what is good in His sight. Whenever we're faced with an
enemy, God will win; we will win with God.

May we be encouraged and filled with courage today
and always. And as we are filled with courage, may we
inspire others.

Prayer: Dear Lord, we pray for Your courage to face our days.
We pray for You to fill us with Your strength to face our
enemies. Things may not always go as we'd like, but You are
always there for us. Thank You.

DAY 24

Grace in Our Challenges

And He said to me, "My grace is sufficient for you, for
My strength is made perfect in weakness." Therefore
most gladly I will rather boast in my infirmities,
that the power of Christ may rest upon me.
—2 Corinthians 12:9

We all experience challenges, "infirmities," but God wants
to use us in spite of them. He wants to display His power
and His strength in our lives in spite of those problems that
don't seem to get any better. He knows that they keep us
dependent on Him, keep us on our knees, crying out to Him,
sometimes daily. He knows. And He wants to perfect His
strength in our weaknesses.

In the end, we will see that it was all for our good. We
will understand that He is truly sovereign and does all things
well. We would have embraced His grace for our lives and
been quieted by His peace. In the end, His strength would
have been made perfect in our weaknesses.

Prayer: Dear Lord, You understand the challenges we
experience. You know me. Lord, please strengthen me to
continue on despite my "infirmities." Please fill me with
Your Spirit and Your grace. Please perfect me as only You
can. And please keep me until You come for us.

DAY 25

Jesus Is Coming Again

Who also said, "Men of Galilee, why do you stand
gazing up into heaven? This same Jesus, who was
taken up from you into heaven, will so come in
like manner as you saw Him go into heaven."
—Acts 1:11

What a wonderful promise! He ascended into heaven, and
He will descend back to us. Until then, just as the early
disciples received the Holy Spirit to empower them to live
as God would have them, we too can be daily refreshed and
empowered by the Holy Spirit to live a life pleasing and
honoring God. He will return. We can be certain of that. We
can be encouraged by that. We can be strengthened by that.

Our Lord and Savior will come again! May we all be
ready.

Prayer: Dear Jesus, thank You for the promise of Your
imminent return. Thank You for Your strength and
encouragement. Lord, hold us in the palms of Your hands
until we meet in the clouds of heaven. Amen.

DAY 26

Perfect Peace

You will keep him in perfect peace, whose mind is stayed on You, because he trusts in You. Trust in the Lord forever, for in Yah, the Lord, is everlasting strength.
—Isaiah 26:3–4

This is a familiar promise to many. Perfect peace. Focus on God. Trust in Him and His everlasting strength. As we encounter life's perplexities and difficulties, may we keep our focus on God and what He would have us to do. (It really does make a difference.) And then may we follow through on what He impresses upon us. This is the way to go.

When we focus on Him, and not on our challenges, we find that our minds are renewed and strengthened. We find that the chaos gets order. We find that the loud voices quiet down. We find perfect peace, everlasting strength, and so much more. May we claim His promise today and dwell in peace.

Prayer: Dear Lord, we need Your peace. Peace that You can give that is like none other. Peace that calms our souls. Thank You for Your peace.

DAY 27

Jesus Prays for Us

I do not pray for these alone, but also for those
who will believe in Me through their word.
—John 17:20

John 17 became a favorite passage of mine when I realized that Jesus prayed for me when He was here on this earth. He was praying for the early church disciples, and He was also praying for you and me. That was so comforting to hear. Prayer support from the King of kings and Lord of lords who also as a man daily connected with His Father; who lived here, died, and rose again just for me.

And do you know that we still have this prayer support? Jesus still prays for me even in heaven. He still prays for us all. He's looking down, smiling on us, encouraging us, strengthening us. He's there for us. May we also pray for others. May we also be there for others.

Prayer: Dear Jesus, thank You for loving me. Thank You for praying for me. Thank You for being there for me. We praise You, for You are our Loving Savior who prays for us.

DAY 28

We Are Overcomers

You are of God, little children, and have
overcome them, because He who is in you
is greater than he who is in the world.
—1 John 4:4

We have overcome all the "stuff" of this world through
Christ. He overcame for us that we too may have the victory.
So what's the "stuff"? The craziness, lies, hurt, sorrow,
sadness, death, pain, sickness, problems—all the "stuff" that
is of this world and of the enemy.

We are not of this world. We are of God, and we have
so much to look forward to, including eternity with our
Savior, a beautiful home, eternal peace, everlasting love, and
much more. Indeed God has overcome; He has overcome all.
Praise God for His overcoming power.

Prayer: Dear Lord, thank You for Your overcoming power.
Thank You for Your sustaining power. Thank You for Your
strengthening power. Thank You.

DAY 29

Strength in Stillness

Be still, and know that I am God; I will be exalted
among the nations, I will be exalted in the earth!
—Psalm 46:10

This is another beloved verse. There is strength in stillness. There is strength in stillness before God. There is strength in dependence upon a mighty God. There is strength in God. We are nothing without Him and can do nothing without His power and help. The beautiful thing is that we don't have to do anything without Him. We don't have to live life on our own or in our own strength. We can always open our hearts to Him. We can always have Him in our lives. We can always have His strength.

Yes, we can be still and know that He is our one true God. He is everything we need, and we can rely on Him. He will be there for us every time. He will quiet us with His love.

Prayer: Dear Lord, we praise You and glorify Your name. You are truly our one true God, loving and kind, who gives us strength to continue on. You love us like no other. And You're always there for us. Thank You for being our God, our Lord, our Savior, and our King.

DAY 30

Seeking the Lord

Seek the Lord and His strength; seek His face evermore!
—1 Chronicles 16:11

In everything—the good, the bad, and the not so bad—seek the Lord, seek His Word, seek His promises, and seek His strength. In the confusion of life, seek His peace, seek His wisdom, and seek His quiet. The more we spend time with Him and the more we seek Him, the more of Him we receive and the more He can supernaturally influence and guide our lives.

The New International Version says, "Look to the Lord; seek His face always." May we daily look to our Lord. May we daily look up to Him. May we daily look for Him. May we daily look at Him. May we daily look to our Lord.

Prayer: My Lord, may we always seek Your strength. Have Your way in my life. Fill me with Your strength, Your peace, and Your wisdom. Every day.

DAY 31

Choose Him

The Lord of hosts is with us; the God of Jacob is our refuge.
—Psalm 46:11

Every single day, God is with us. God is our shelter, our safe haven, and our sanctuary. Every day. But we have to choose Him. We have to choose to allow Him into our lives. We have to choose His strength, His shelter, and His power. He's calling out to you with love and compassion. He wants to strengthen you. He wants to empower you. He wants to guide you. Won't you choose Him today and every day? Won't you accept Him into your life today? He is our God of love. He is our help. He is our strength. He is our refuge.

Prayer: Lord, I choose You today and every day. I choose Your strength. I choose Your power. I choose You. Fill me, Lord, today and every day.

Strong is the strength that God supplies,
through His eternal Son.
—Ellen White, *This Day with God*

Printed in the United States
By Bookmasters